WOMEN'S BASEBALL

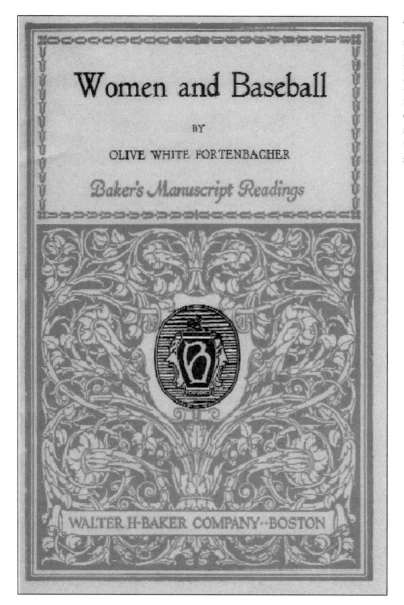

Women and Baseball

BY

OLIVE WHITE FORTENBACHER

Baker's Manuscript Readings

WALTER H·BAKER COMPANY··BOSTON

This is the cover of a two-part baseball monologue written by Olive White Fortenbacher. The monologue is a view of the happenings at a baseball game through the eyes of a woman in 1934.

(*on the cover, front, top left*) Katie Pappa hurls a pitch during the 2002 Great Lakes Women's Baseball Classic. Against the Great Lakes All-Stars, she threw a four hit game, striking out seven and winning 7 to 1. In that game she also went two-for-four and knocked in a pair of runs.

(*front, bottom right*) This photograph was taken during the AAGPBL spring training in Miami, FL. Sliding is Sophie Kurys of Racine and attempting to put the tag on her is Ruth "Tex" Lessing, catcher for Grand Rapids.

(*back cover*) Female players tried to ply their interest in baseball whenever and wherever they could. Pictured here are two players from Texas.

(*background*) See double page spread on pages 34 and 35.

WOMEN'S BASEBALL

John M. Kovach

ARCADIA
PUBLISHING

Published by Arcadia Publishing
Charleston, South Carolina

Printed in the United States of America

Library of Congress Catalog Card Number: 2005920263

For all general information contact Arcadia Publishing at:
Telephone 843-853-2070
Fax 843-853-0044
E-mail sales@arcadiapublishing.com
For customer service and orders:
Toll-Free 1-888-313-2665

Visit us on the Internet at www.arcadiapublishing.com

Baseball

Of all spring sports at Vermont, baseball stands first. It's lots of fun girls to go down to the old diamond at Grassmount two or three times a week for a real live game of baseball. A whiz. A crash. A dash to first base—a pass ball; steal second, and hold your base. A long grounder past center field and a run comes in. How about it, 1931? Won't you too hand out some good stiff opposition in the spring of 1928?

This is a copy of the 1927–28 Vermont College Women's Athletic Association handbook listing for the Baseball Club. The handbook encouraged the women to "choose your athletics with as much care as you do your studies."

CONTENTS

ACKNOWLEDGMENTS

When I first got involved with women's baseball back in 1991, I quickly learned that there was a huge segment of the population who were not allowed to dream or follow their dreams of playing baseball because of their gender. Since that time, I never try to miss an opportunity to make the case why girls and women should have the same baseball (and other) opportunities as males.

I would like to thank John Pearson and the whole Arcadia editorial staff for believing that this pictorial would have wide appeal. It's not meant to be a dissertation on women's baseball; rather, through the images that have been collected, it's meant to show how we *already* identify girls and women as baseball players and have done so for nearly 140 years in books, magazines, movies, and artwork. Yet, the *opportunity to play* baseball is still a major obstacle for many who love the game.

A special thanks as always, goes to my family—wife Lisa and daughters Emily, Irina, and Marina. You've always got my back!

Thanks as well go to my co-workers at both Saint Mary's College and the St. Joseph County Public Library.

Thanks to Carrie Pappa and the wonderful images of women's baseball she has provided these past three seasons and to all the players who sent their photographs.

And finally, a special thanks to all of my players, past, present, and future…and your love of the game.

INTRODUCTION

To take you into the history, present, and future of women's baseball, two wonderful young women, Katie Pappa and Molly McKesson, tell why baseball is important to them and why they play the game.

I don't remember not playing baseball. My parents say that I grew up in the dugout. I have two older brothers, John and Danny. John is eight years older than me. John's team taught me to spit sunflower seeds in the dugout when I was two. By the time I was four, I would spend hours tossing the ball up and hitting it like I had seen my dad do at the ball field. Our Labrador was happy to spend all day bringing the ball back for me to hit it again.

I guess I really started playing baseball out of convenience. When Danny was seven, my dad was the President of the league and coached Danny's team while my mom kept the scorebook in the dugout. They signed me up to play on Danny's Little League team when I was five so that I would be allowed in the dugout during the games. There was a pond next to our baseball field and my parents were always afraid I would wander off and drown! If I was playing ball, at least they would know where I was.

Some people thought I should have been playing softball with the other girls (mostly softball coaches!), but my parents were not about to take on another schedule with softball. I always had a lot of support playing baseball from my coaches, teammates, and their families. I was lucky to have good coaches who stressed solid fundamentals. It was never about being a girl playing on a boy's team. It was about playing baseball.

I played baseball every summer through Babe Ruth League. I started playing on the South Bend Blue Sox, a women's baseball team, when I was 13. It's fun to play in a league with all women players. We play baseball because we love the game.

Katie Pappa/South Bend Blue Sox

Baseball is like no other sport. You have to be physically fit, but most of all, mentally prepared—especially being a pitcher.

I started playing baseball when I was watching my dad and brother practice. I decided to give it a try myself and loved it! Since I was eight years old, one of my goals was to play college baseball. Now 10 years later, after hard work, dedication and love for the game, I made my dream a reality. I'm the first girl to receive an NCAA baseball scholarship. I'm looking forward to my first college season this spring at Christian Brothers University, a Division II school in Memphis, Tennessee.

If I were to say one thing to young girls who are interested in playing baseball, it would be that you are constantly under a microscope. Whatever you do, good or bad, is magnified times ten. There will always be politics wherever you play, but the key is to keep improving your game and it will eventually pay off. Don't listen to naysayers who will try to persuade you to switch to softball—it is a totally different game.

Hopefully, women's baseball will soon become an Olympic sport and more young girls will be playing the wonderful sport of baseball at all levels.

Molly McKesson/Ocala, FL Lightning

ONE

The Early Days 1866–1900

Vassar College. Anyway you look at it women's baseball owes its beginnings to the creative young women of Vassar College in 1866.

The idea of females playing baseball might not have had the chance to even get off the ground had the idea not happened at a women's college. Other women's colleges followed suit including Smith College in 1879, Mount Holyoke in 1891, Wellesley in 1897, and Saint Mary's College in 1905.

Perceptions of women being weak, passive, or frail were soon dispelled at these institutions. All of the students, in addition to the academic rigors, were required to participate in exercise, and so it was only natural that other avenues of athletic participation would soon result.

Although this activity in baseball was active and growing on the grounds of these early pioneers, the baseball play was usually done in a fairly secluded spot and thus it did not draw too much attention from the outside world.

Those early players had another obstacle to overcome—one which today we would never even give much thought to. Imagine players of today after hitting the ball or running after a ball on defense, having about 30 extra pounds of long clothing that would have to be lifted and carried on your way to first base or while tracking down a grounder or fly ball!

During the later part of the 1860s, the first play of an African-American women's team was noted. In 1867, just one year after women took to the diamond at Vassar, the Dolly Vardens played in the Philadelphia area. Their uniforms consisted of long red calico dresses.

It was only natural that by the mid-1870s the interest of women wanting to play baseball would continue to grow. In 1875, the first female baseball players to play for money took to the field in Springfield, Illinois. Two teams, known as the Blondes and Brunettes, would travel to large cities like Chicago and New York. They would also travel to smaller communities like South Bend, Indiana. In September of 1883, the local baseball management told the Blondes and Brunettes that they could not find an open date for the team to play. According to the local baseball management, "All dates for the South Bend ball grounds are filled and the mayor does not permit playing in the city park." However, two years later, the Blondes and Brunettes finally got an open date at Island Park. Nevertheless, they were coming to the end of their touring days.

Perhaps one of the biggest innovations for the female players was the advent of an outfit that would make playing the games somewhat easier. As mentioned earlier, the long-skirted ballplayers found out their cumbersome clothing slowed down the play of the game. Amelia Bloomer was an early pioneer in the struggle for women's rights. Beginning in the late 1840s, she espoused the wearing of a rather loose-fitting trouser based on the design of a similar undergarment created by Elizabeth Smith Miller.

Often referred to as Bloomers, the outfit was highly controversial and many in the women's movement in the 1840s and 1850s chose not to follow the lead of Bloomer in wearing such an outfit. However, while not an acceptable fashion away from the baseball diamond, the bloomers became the fashion of the diamond. The name became synonymous with female baseball players for nearly 40 years, and the players were known as "Bloomer Girls."

This 1887 magazine illustration depicts a young girl playing baseball with the boys. Undoubtedly, the caption "A Scratch Nine" refers to the boys having to use a girl in order to be able to play that day.

In terms of women's baseball, Vassar College is considered the beginning point in history. The first organized games there took place in 1866, almost 140 years ago. This postcard from the early 1900s is a reminder of those early days.

In this image, an early women's baseball team is depicted wearing striped uniform pants and a rather large hat. The players on both ends of the back row have a baseball in their hand.

COMING
SUNDAY, AUG. 9,
AT
Island Park!
YOUNG LADIES
Base Ball Club,
Blondes and Brunettes. The Champion Female Base Ball Players of the World.
THE YOUNG LADIES' CLUB
VS.
A Picked Nine of Young Men.

Never here before, may never be again. Don't fail to see this game. Exciting to the highest degree. Your only chance. Only organization of the kind in the world. Sensation of the day. Immense crowds everywhere. Ladies especially invited. Don't miss it. The only opportunity of a lifetime to see them play. Game called at 3:30 p. m.

In 1883, a visit by a women's baseball team was turned down by the local baseball management in South Bend, Indiana. Two years later, an advertisement in the *South Bend Daily Times* announced an August 9 visit to the city by the "Blondes and Brunettes." The women played a "picked nine" from South Bend and played before a crowd of 1,000. The visitors fell by a score of 15 to 7. Nearly 60 years later, South Bend would have its own professional women's baseball club, the Blue Sox of the All-American Girls Professional Baseball League.

This October 14, 1882 issue of *The National Police Gazette* shows the interest in baseball by the women fans of that period. Whether standing on a barrel for a better view or peeking through a knothole in the outfield, it shows that love for and interest in baseball transcends gender.

A young female ballplayer is all set to play baseball with her mitt, bat, and ball in hand. This rendering is from *The Youth's Companion* and is dated April 11, 1898.

The Girls Play To-Day

BOSTON BLOOMERS

Ladies

CHAMPION

BASE BALL CLUB

Of the World

✳✳✳✳✳

In their
Twentieth
Century
Uniforms.

Greatest
Novelty
of the Age.

✳✳✳✳✳

In an Interesting, Exciting and Scientific Game against a Local Club of this City. ❧ ❧ ❧ ❧

A High Class, Moral Amusement

Patronized by the BEST PEOPLE Everywhere.

Plenty of Good Seats and Shade   Come and Bring the Ladies

GAME CALLED AT 3.

This type of advertising handbill was used by the Bloomer teams when they traveled to different cities. Note the wording that refers to the Bloomers as "A High Class Moral Amusement" and "Greatest Novelty of the Age."

14

Two

Bloomers and Beyond
1900–1942

In the 1890s through the 1930s, many if not most of the female baseball teams were known by the catchy "Bloomer Girls" name. It did not matter if they were from New York, Chicago, or even Boston, the Bloomer Girls name became the tag synonymous with women's baseball.

Now the Bloomer Girls' teams (at least a number of them) did not always find themselves comprised of all females. In many of the photographs of teams from that era, including a number of those featured in this book, a careful look will find a male or two in the team photograph.

Depending on the team, the males might pitch and catch, or catch and play first base, and so on. It may be hard to believe now, but even baseball Hall of Famers "Smoky" Joe Wood and Rogers Hornsby spent some of their younger days playing for Bloomer Girls' teams. Called "toppers," the male players would often wear wigs and a skirt to blend in with their teammates.

Very rarely (if at all) did the Bloomer Girls play each other. Rather, their season was that of a barnstorming nature, traversing across various parts of the United States, playing in big cities and little towns. Their opposition would be that of the local strong amateur, semi-pro or even in some cases, all-star "picked nine" teams.

One of the most important figures from this time period was Maud Nelson. A fine ballplayer in her own right, Nelson would be one of the figures who would keep baseball opportunities open for females through the mid-1930s.

Her earliest success in the owner, promoter, and manager role was with the Western Bloomer Girls. She would also go on to operate the American Athletic Girls and the All-Star Rangers. Many said that of all of the Bloomer teams around, the best two were the New York Bloomers run by Margaret Nabel and the Western Bloomers of Nelson.

Nelson was one of the first team operators to also start outfitting her team in regular baseball uniforms and dropping the "Bloomer" name, which had originally gained notoriety for the teams. While many of the teams recruited close to their main area of operation, Nelson would pick up talent from nearby Chicago, as well as in smaller towns along the way!

On one of Nelson's final All-Star Rangers teams was Rose Gacioch. She was an excellent ballplayer, and playing for the Rangers was just the beginning. She would go on to play in the All-American Girls Professional Baseball League.

By the middle of the 1930s, an ebb in female baseball activity would take place. Softball was starting to encroach into its territory. Many athletic journals and publications began to say that female athletes were not capable of playing regulation baseball. They were not strong enough to make the long throws across the diamond; overhand pitching put too much of a strain on their arms, and so on.

It was this combination of events that has so ingrained the idea into society that men play baseball and women play softball.

There were many though, who would not let the dream of playing baseball die. Whether on sandlots or on semi-pro teams, all across the United States, women would continue to uphold the tradition of women in baseball set by Vassar in 1866. Their reward was a professional league that would change the face of the female athlete forever.

THE WESTERN BLOOMER GIRLS—LADIES' CHAMPION BASE BALL CLUB

This postcard is of the Western Bloomer Girls Baseball team made famous by Maud Nelson (pictured at far left in the front row). Cards like this one were often used to promote the traveling Bloomer teams.

BASE BALL

BOSTON

BLOOMER

GIRLS

PLAY TODAY

Admission 25 cents

GRAND STAND EXTRA

SEE OTHER SIDE

This is the front side of the handbill (dated *c.* 1900) that was used to help promote the Boston Bloomer Girls' team. The Bloomer teams were very similar to the barnstorming men's baseball teams that would go from town to town and play a local team or all-star aggregation.

EVENTS.

I. Running High Jump.

B. L. DeGraff, 1900.
R. Wells, 1900.
E. L. Johnson, 1900.
V. Barnard, 1900.

E. M. Garvin, 1901.
E. H. White, 1902.
H. M. McWilliams, 1903.

1st................................2d..................................3d...............................Height...........

II. Throwing the Base Ball.

E. Bradley, 1900.
M. B. Comstock, 1900.
H. B. Long, 1900.
M. F. Jackson, 1901.
G. P. Burleigh, 1901.
J. B. Lockwood, 1901.

E. M. Garvin, 1901.
E. T. Corrigan, 1902.
D. E. Merrill, 1902.
A. M. Cuddeback, 1902.
M. H. McDonald, 1903.

1st.............................2d................................3d...........................Distance..........

III. 100-Yard Dash. Trials.

1. L. S. Holmquist, 1901.
   L. H. Barbour, 1902.
   A. L. Kellogg, 1903.

2. G. Bruce, 1902.
   K. M. Morgan, 1903.
   E. S. Jackson, 1903.

3. A. M. Burnham, 1900.
   G. D. Scott, 1901.

4. B. L. DeGraff, 1900.
   L. B. Platt, 1901.
   H. Gross, 1901.

1st heat won by...Time...........................

2d heat won by...Time...........................

3d heat won by...Time...........................

4th heat won by..Time...........................

IV. Throwing the Basket Ball.

E. Bradley, 1900.
L. S. Bartlett, 1900.
M. B. Comstock, 1900.
E. M. Garvin, 1901.
J. Pulsifer, 1901.

M. Calhoun, 1901.
H. Stewart, 1901.
E. H. White, 1902.
A. M. Cuddeback, 1902.
A. S. Wood, 1903.

1st..............................2d................................3d...........................Distance..........

Even when not fielding baseball teams, Vassar College kept their ties to the sport by having as part of its Field Day a "Throwing the Base Ball" event. As noted in this 1900 Field Day program, there were contestants from all four class years at Vassar competing in this event.

The Chicago Ladies Base Ball Club is pictured here, c. 1902. In the early 1900s, female baseball teams like this one from Chicago would travel in geographic regions of 200 miles of more showcasing their baseball skills. The strong baseball tradition continues for Chicago as two clubs (the Storm and Gems) are members of the Great Lakes Women's Baseball League. The Chicago Storm won the AAU Women's National Baseball Championship in 2003.

LODA WILL BE HERE

With Her Ball Team

FRIDAY, JULY 28, '05

To Play The

SHELDON STARS

SHELDON BALL PARK

The Umpire will call Game at 2:15 sharp.   Admission 25c.

There were large numbers of women's baseball teams cropping up in the early 1900s. Much of the history of those teams has become lost over the years. Some unique pieces of their history have survived, as evidenced by this 1905 handbill featuring "Loda and Her Ball Team."

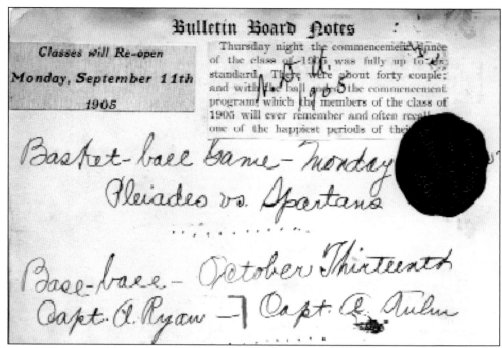

This Bulletin Board Note from Saint Mary's College in Notre Dame, Indiana, is announcing a Base-Ball game that is to take place on October 13, 1905. Like many of the other women's colleges, baseball was a popular sport at Saint Mary's. This image is from the scrapbook of Agnes Kuhn, class of 1907. She was designated as one of the team captains for the game. (Images reproduced from Agnes Kuhn Scrapbook/Saint Mary's College Archives, Notre Dame, Indiana.)

Besides flyers and postcards announcing their arrival into town, some of the Bloomer Girls teams would travel with their own band. Many times the band would lead them into the town and to the ballpark for the games that day. This postcard is of the Star Bloomer Club of Indianapolis, Indiana.

This September 6, 1907 newspaper clipping from the *South Bend News-Times* tells of an early African-American women's baseball club from the Kansas City, Missouri area. Like many articles of that era reporting women's baseball, a fair part of the stories were usually spent describing the outfits of the team.

This postcard features the New York Bloomer Girls team of Margaret Nabel (#10 in the photograph). It was through the efforts, organization and business skills of Nabel and Maud Nelson that made their teams the best of women's baseball from that era.

BALL TEAM OF NEGRO GIRLS.

Stranger Sees Practice of Aggregation of Colored Female Athletes.

Kansas City, Mo.—A man was strolling toward the baseball field on the Parade at dusk recently.

A group of dark figures were playing ball on the diamond.

"That's right, Fannie, put 'em over the plate!"

"All right, May, look at this."

"Heavens!" exclaimed the man. "What names for ball players."

He hastened around the field and came within full view of the players.

Out in the field was a full team of negro girls, ranging in age from 18 to 22 years, clad in short blue skirts, white shirt waists, black stockings, and regulation baseball shoes. They were equipped with every modern device for capturing the frisky baseball.

LEFT TO RIGHT—9-Ethel Condon; 8-Toots Andr==; 1-Helen Demarest; 3-Peggy Rohr; 7-"Babe" McCutton; 6-Ruth Doyle; 6-Evelyn Lynch; 5 Rose Roth; 4-Florrie O'Rourke; 10-Margaret Nabel, Manager

This is another style of promotional postcards used by the Bloomer Girls teams. Many of these cards would carry the contact information for the team. This particular New York Bloomer team was based out of Brooklyn, New York.

New York Bloomer Girls
...Champion...
Female Baseball Players of the World

N. Y. BLOOMER GIRLS	AB	R	H	PO	A	E		AR	R	H	PO	A	E
Agnes Parker, 2b													
Caroline Andres, ss													
Estelle Prins, p													
Chester Prins, c													
Florence Van Derburc, 1b													
Alma Pape, rf													
Mae Sleichar, lf													
Loretta Stanley, cf													
Mildred Van Darwall, p													
Carrie Stumph, of													
J. McCann,													

On the backs of many postcards produced for the Bloomer teams, fans would find a scorecard. Sometimes the scorecards would be blank when listing the visiting Bloomer teams (as in the case of the one shown here); other times, the line-up would be pre-printed on the scorecard.

22

Greetings from
The Boston Bloomer Girls

Many of the Bloomer teams would carry anywhere from two to four men on their roster as pictures in some of the previous postcards show. However, this Boston Bloomer Girls team depicts only women on their roster. Note the rather large lettering on the front of their uniforms.

NATIONA

This is the 1915 National B.B.C. (Baseball Club) of Holyoke, Massachusetts. One of their players, Tillie Bergeron (first row, second from right) never told her family that she had played

B.C.

on this team. After her death, the photograph was discovered in her attic and a family member recognized her.

Images of females participating in baseball were continually used on postcards, although many were artistic renderings rather than actual photographs. Here, a young woman is about to catch a baseball and the caption is playing on the baseball term "liner to" and the words, "line or two."

This image of an African-American female player, "The Base Ball-Girl," complete with poem, carries a postmark from 1917. This postcard was far more stereotypical in its portrayal than the image at the top of this page.

In 1915, Saint Mary's College junior Dympna Balbach captured some of the festivities associated with baseball games on the campus. Some of the women pictured here are fans wearing large letters on their backs, along with some uniquely styled hats, to root on their respective teams. (Image reproduced from Dympna Balbach Collection/Saint Mary's College Archives, Notre Dame, Indiana.)

Here is a group of young female baseball players, c. 1915. All appear to be wearing some sort of insignia on their hats. It's very possible that this is some sort of a school field day activity.

A young female pitcher kicks and delivers to home plate as crowds on both sides of the field watch. This image was taken in 1917, at Aloha Hive in South Fairlee, Vermont. Notice the umpire in the picture standing behind the pitcher, wearing a tie.

A group of female baseball players from Jeannette, PA, take time to gather for a photograph on a front porch. This photograph was taken in August of 1913.

From the lettering on their uniform, it appears that these two female players are members of their high school baseball team. Notice the baseball grip of the player on the left and the glove worn by her teammate.

This is a view from the outfield toward the grandstand during a women's baseball game in 1922. The game was played at Pine Tree Camp in Pocono Pines, PA. The image shows a base runner making a break toward second base.

A base runner falls just short of her destination and is tagged out by a fielder. It's evident from the photograph that although the "play" is being staged, the participants seem to be enjoying being part of this baseball scene.

Here is a studio image of a female Bloomer Girl. With hands split in Ty-Cobb fashion, she appears to be waiting for her pitch. Note the "B" on her sleeve that is surrounded by a baseball diamond outline.

Female players tried to ply their interest in baseball whenever and wherever they could. Pictured here are two players from Texas. The skirted hitter awaits a pitch while a well-equipped catcher stands behind her. In the background, a young boy takes in the action.

Blanche Adelia Hazel Vey Mary Bessie Amy Helen Bertha.

The front porch is again the backdrop for this young women's baseball team from Spencer, IA. According to the back of the photograph, they play for the high school team (as evidenced by the "S" in the baseball diamond on their sleeve). The photograph dates to *c.* 1910.

Ruth Carlson, the sender of this postcard, asks the recipient, Mr. A. Berg, if he likes their baseball team. Taken in 1914, the photograph shows a game in progress with the fans or extra players in close proximity to the field.

This is the Speedy Maroon Busters women's baseball club from Minnesota. Unlike many of the female teams from this era, they chose not to have "Bloomer Girls" in any part of their name. This unique moniker is based on this photograph showing the dark or "maroon" color of their uniforms. You'll also notice the triple overlay of the letters "S, M," and "B" (Speedy Maroon Busters) that appears on their left chest.

The group of young women pictured here are part of the Andover and Weston (Vermont) Girls Baseball Team. This photograph was taken in 1913. Their uniforms feature players wearing large "A's" or "W's" right in the middle of their blouses.

Taken in New York in 1918, this photograph shows a series of different women's baseball games being played at the same time. The game in the foreground shows a pitcher delivering a pitch to

the batter while the umpire (with white shirt and tie) stands behind her. This photograph could be part of a play or field day, or possibly a tournament.

The June 14, 1913 cover of the *Saturday Evening Post* shows a young girl headed off to play baseball while a young boy sits and pouts. The *Post* was one of the publications that used images of female baseball players in a number of different decades.

This is a postcard shows a female ballplayer with the letters "CBC" on her uniform. The card has an embossed design with its greeting of "With Best Wishes" written in gold script.

This images shows a male ballplayer pictured with two female baseball players. The two females are wearing the same type of jersey, while the male player (with baseball in hand) appears to be the "opposing" pitcher.

Taken from the 1927–28 *Vermont College Women's Athletic Association Handbook*, this picture shows a baseball game in progress. It was noted in the handbook that of all the spring sports, "baseball stands first."

FIG. 15. COMPLETING THE SWING

In the 1920s, there were a number of different instructional books written about how to develop skills in baseball for both girls and women. This picture shows one of the hitters in the 1929 book *Baseball For Girls and Women*, which was written by Gladys E. Palmer, assistant professor of physical education at Ohio State University.

FIG. 18. FINISH OF THE OVERHAND.
Flexion of the wrist at this point gives additional speed.

Also taken from the *Baseball For Girls and Women* publication is this photograph of a player completing her throw. Books like this one would not only show technique, but would also consist of different types of drills to develop baseball skills.

Here is a studio photograph taken of a female baseball pitcher. This image was taken in Cleveland, Ohio, around 1918. Her glove appears to be a finger model with the fingers not being laced together.

YOUNG WOMEN FORM HOME BASEBALL TEAM

GETTYSBURG. S. D.. July 6.— Twenty young women of Gettysburg have organized a baseball team which they claim to be the only team of exclusively home talent feminine players in the world.

This appeared in the *South Bend News-Times* on July 7, 1915, and details (with great enthusiasm) the start-up of a "home-grown" women's baseball team in Gettysburg, South Dakota, with 20 players making up its roster.

These three Elkhart, Indiana women look like they are ready to play ball. One player is getting in some practice work on shielding her eyes from the sun, as the photographer on that day appears to have them all looking into a bright sun.

Sixteen-year-old Elizabeth "Babe" Lasocki created quite a stir in Chicopee, MA, in March of 1937, when she stated she wanted to try out for the high school baseball team. The principle of the school was adamantly against her playing.

Just as indoor baseball was a way for their male counterparts on the diamond to stay in condition over the winter, so it was for the Federal Rubber Company team of Milwaukee, WI, in 1923–24. The team captured the Milwaukee City Championship that winter.

Helen Carson, a resident of Middleton, CT, was named as the starting pitcher for a Britton Woods, NH, 1938 summer resort baseball team. The 19-year-old pitcher threw both slow and fast curves, and dropped balls, and was a switch hitter at bat. Newspapers at the time said that she was a great all-around athlete and would be the successor to "Babe" Didrickson.

In 1929, the Founder's Day activities at Vassar College included, yes, you guessed it—baseball. In this photograph a player awaits for action at the "hot corner."

Also taken during the 1929 Founder's Day at Vassar is a photograph of a batter poking a hit to the outfield. When the two photographs on this page were taken, it had been over 60 years since the first baseball games were played at Vassar.

Often outstanding female players would carry their own advertising…mainly their names on the front of their uniforms. One such player was Maggie Riley. In this 1927 photograph, Riley leaps to snare a line drive. She was often referred to in the press as a "Babe Ruth at bat."

This is an August, 1930 program cover for the Cleveland, Ohio Barth Gems Girls Indoor Baseball Team. The program lists their game versus the Rochester, New York Police Department, which would be played in Red Wing Stadium. The team was extremely popular in the Cleveland area and traveled both in the Midwest and in eastern parts of the United States.

The Cleveland
Barth Gem Girls Baseball Team
Ate Our Famous
75c Roast Chicken Dinner Today
Ford Cafeteria
67 Chestnut Street

Looking through the program for the Cleveland Barth Gems Indoor Baseball team, it's very easy to see how popular they were in their community. Many of the ads (such as this one) promote the local businesses and how good they are based on the fact that the Barth Gems ate, stayed at, or used their products!

Pictured here is a young woman who is playing infield at a ball diamond that seems to be in a large city (based upon the buildings in the background). This photograph, taken c. 1922, has her wearing the "bloomer" type pants as part of her uniform.

This news article appeared in the *South Bend News-Times* on May 23, 1931, and mentions that the Colored Bloomer Girl team of Jerry Goodwin is the "only one of its kind in the country." They, like the other Bloomer teams, would spend most of their time on the road.

GIRLS' NINE AT GALIEN MONDAY

GALIEN, Mich., May 23. — Jerry Goodwin and his Colored Bloomer Girl Baseball club, the only one of its kind in the country, will play three games in Michigan this year, one with the Galien Rogers here next Monday.

Having proper equipment is important for any baseball player. In this photograph, a young female ballplayer is a carrying a brand new Wilson catcher's mask out to the field of play.

Miss Hilda Ferris, a graduate of Bryn Mawr and athletic director of the Friends School in Moorestown, NJ, brought girls baseball to the school. In this photograph, Katherine Graff is shown sliding while Helen Holmes (playing second base) puts the tag on her.

In 1929, 15-year-old outfielder Alice Buckman beat out nine boys for a spot on the Griswold, IA high school baseball team. It was noted that she made this team the first year she was able to try out.

Nineteen-year-old catcher Vada Corbus signed a contract with the minor league Joplin (MO) Miners in 1931. According to newspaper reports, her only drawback was that she weighed only 115 pounds, but her knowledge and skills and box office value would make her an asset to the team.

What's right with
when gi

Starting in the teens and later, many companies used girls playing baseball to promote their products. This ad for P and G Soap appeared in *Ladies' Home Journal* in September of 1931. It

he world
just *will* be boys?

shows a young girl from Portsmouth, OH, completing a skirts-high, hard slide into home plate.

Another 1931 magazine cover of a young girl sliding into a base appeared in May of that year on *Liberty Magazine*. The young skirted girl slides to avoid a throw that has not yet reached its target.

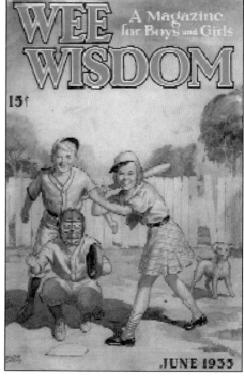

The June 1935 issue of *Wee Wisdom* depicts yet another young girl playing baseball. With bat in hand, she appears to be looking for a pitch she can drive to the gaps. It is interesting to see that the boys in the picture have on baseball shoes, but the young girl seems to be wearing a dress shoe.

Perhaps no female baseball player made more of a name for herself in the 1930s than Jackie Mitchell. In 1931, Mitchell signed with the Chattanooga Lookouts as a 17-year-old left-handed pitcher. In an exhibition game versus the New York Yankees, she fanned Babe Ruth and Lou Gehrig. However, her minor league career was short-lived as then baseball commissioner Kenesaw Mountain Landis voided her contract as the grounds that life in baseball for her would be "too strenuous."

NIGHT BASEBALL

HOUSE OF DAVID PARK

BENTON HARBOR, MICH.

Saturday Night, Aug. 26
8:30 P. M.

HOUSE OF DAVID
EASTERN STATES
TRAVELING CLUB

— vs. —

HOUSE OF DAVID
CENTRAL STATES
TRAVELING CLUB

Featuring Jackie Mitchell,
19-year-old girl pitching
sensation.

This ad is from the *South Bend News-Times* of August 24, 1933. The House of David was a well-known barnstorming team of that era and one of their headliners in the upcoming contest was a 19-year-old pitcher by the name of Jackie Mitchell.

After her brief fling with minor league baseball in Chattanooga, Jackie Mitchell became the first female player for the famous House of David Baseball Team. In this photograph, Jackie is showing her pitching grip to teammates Harry Laufer (center) and George Anderson.

The Spalding Athletic Library produced this publication about outdoor baseball for girls and women from the 1930 season. Like many similar publications, this book would describe methods of instruction for organizing and teaching the skills of baseball. The most up to date rules would also be included.

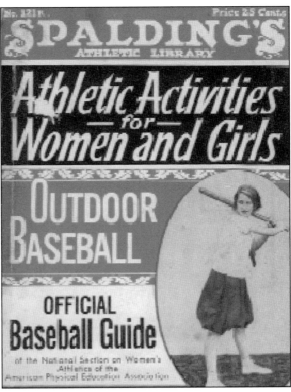

This September 2, 1939 issue of *Collier's* shows a rather determined young female baseball player hitting the ball hard, much to the surprise of the young boy in back of the plate. *Collier's* was just another of the magazine's to feature girls playing baseball as artwork on its cover.

55

KENESAW MOUNTAIN LANDIS,
Commissioner of Base Ball.

Inside the cover of the 1933 *Spalding Guide* was a wonderful letter from then Baseball Commissioner Kenesaw Mountain Landis. In this letter, Landis touted the fact that he hoped that young women would play baseball as widely as it was played by young men. The letter is

FOREWORD

From the Commissioner of Baseball,
Hon. KENESAW M. LANDIS.

It is significant that baseball has retained the place it has in the hearts of sport-loving Americans throughout the half century and more of its existence as a competitive sport. Millions of our young men have played it and the spirit of sportsmanship it inculcates as well as the physical and mental alertness it develops have been no small factor in promoting good citizenship. It is indeed a wonderful thing that these benefits may now be enjoyed by our girls and young women under the supervision of properly constituted authorities on women's athletics. As a sport for women it should adapt itself admirably to the athletic programs of playgrounds, schools and colleges everywhere. It is easy to learn and enjoyment and practical benefits may be derived from playing it regardless of the player's skill. I hope to see baseball played as widely by young women in the years to come as it is by young men today.

interesting from the standpoint that Landis, just two years earlier, had voided the minor league baseball contract of Jackie Mitchell.

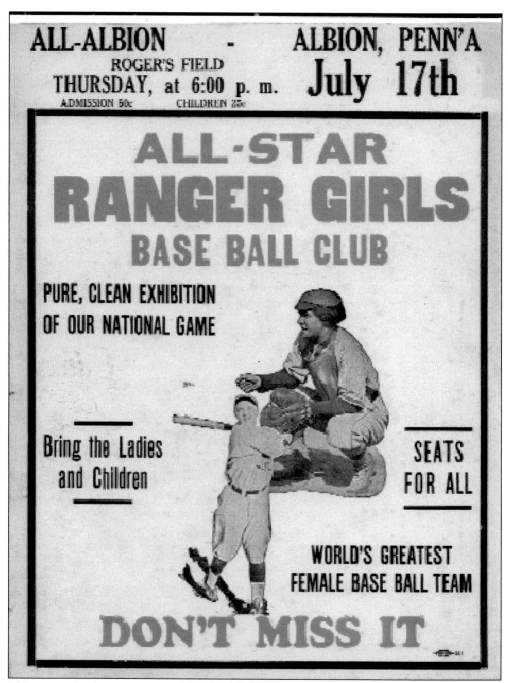

This promotional poster was used by the All-Star Rangers Women's Baseball Club for a July 17 game at Rogers Field in Albion, PA. Maud Nelson, who organized a number of different women's baseball teams in the early 1900s, was co-owner and manger of this club as well. One of her top players was a youngster named Rosie Gacioch. Although she did not play a long time for the Rangers (1934 was their final year), she did use her experience to gain a spot in the All-American Girls Professional Baseball League in 1944.

The August 10, 1940 *Saturday Evening Post* featured a young baseball hitter on its cover. The pig-tailed girl awaits a pitch while standing over an old wooden home plate.

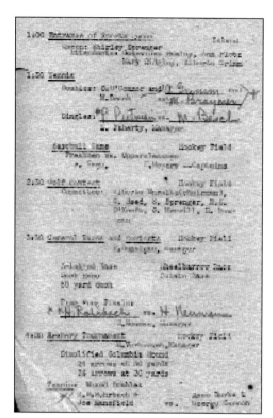

As part of the 1935 Sports Day activity at Saint Mary's College, a baseball game featuring the freshman versus a combination team made up of sophomores, juniors and seniors took place. The freshman team was managed by Rosemary Page, and the upper class team was managed by Katherine Myers. (Image reproduced from the Women's Athletic Association Collection, Saint Mary's College Archives, Notre Dame, Indiana.)

Many times throughout the years, there would be baseball throwing contests for girls. Sometimes they would be for distance, other times they would be for accuracy. Pictured here is a bracelet with charms won by a young woman with a pretty good arm. All three charms have a baseball pitcher on the front. Two charms show the 1940 and 1941 first place awards for the baseball throwing event.

THREE

The All Americans
1942–1957

As the threat of World War II threatened to suspend play in the major leagues, Chicago Cub owner Philip Wrigley had a plan. He wanted to keep baseball being played in Wrigley Field even if the major leagues were shut down. With the help of Cub assistant general manager Ken Sells and the flamboyant Branch Rickey, a plan was hatched to operate a women's professional ball league.

The league would use shorter pitching distances and base paths along with underhanded pitching with a 12-inch ball. Yet, players would be allowed to lead off and steal. It was truly a hybrid between baseball and softball. By its final season, however, a regulation size baseball was used along with 85-foot base paths and a 60-foot pitching distance.

Wrigley would also mandate that all the players in the league be as feminine as a pin-up girls, yet be able to play ball like a major leaguer. To ensure the femininity for the players, the entire league would play in skirted uniforms and attend charm school! A number of former major leaguers managed during the life of the league including baseball Hall of Famers Max Carey and Jimmie Foxx. Carey would also serve the league as president in the late 1940s.

In May of 1943, the cities of Kenosha and Racine, WI, along with South Bend, IN, and Rockford, IL, became the first teams to bring Wrigley's dream to reality as the All-American Girls Professional Baseball League (AAGPBL). On July 1, 1943, players from the league would play the historic first night game in Wrigley Field! Over the course of its 12-year life (the final season was 1954), over 14 cities in the Midwest were home to AAGPBL franchises. Only Rockford and South Bend, however, were members for its duration.

Salaries in the AAGPBL ranged from $50 to $125 per week. At that time, the average wage earner was making around $40 per week.

Wrigley, however, was only part of the league the first two seasons. Once it was evident that World War II would not close down the major leagues, he sold the league to Chicago advertising executive Arthur Meyerhoff. Under Meyerhoff, the greatest expansion and success of the league was reached.

Whether it was spring training in Cuba (where the AAGPBL outdrew many of the major league teams who were there at the same time); to its expansion to 10 teams that drew nearly one million paying fans in 1948; to making the ball smaller, the baselines and pitching distances longer, and moving from the underhand to sidearm to overhand pitching, the successes of Meyerhoff were countless.

However, many clubs felt that his idea of "spending money to make more money" was not what they wanted. So, after the 1950 season, local communities took over tasks that once fell upon a well-oiled, centralized league office. Coupled with the end of World War II, gas rationing, and other forms of entertainment like television, the locally managed clubs limped through their final seasons.

Following the 1954 season (which almost was never played), league directors decided to "suspend play" for 1955 to examine their options and regroup. When that did not happen, a number of players and coaches put together a team that traveled like the old-time Bloomer Girls teams of days gone by. Finally, after a three-year run, the story of the All-American Girls Professional Baseball League came to a close. The final appearance of players from the AAGPBL was on August 28, 1957, when the barnstorming All-Americans played the South Bend Blue Sox at Playland Park. Some 2,000 fans witnessed this last historical game.

Many things were left behind including the wonderful memories of those who grew up watching the women play baseball. Many players remained as members of the communities where they used to play. In Fort Wayne, a girl's baseball program still exists, the oldest such program in the United States.

The 12 years of the AAGPBL laid ground work for the female athletes of today. The movie A League of Their Own brought recognition after many years to these pioneer players and launched a whole new legion of fans.

Even though its membership of players is slowly starting to fade away, an All-American Girls Players Association was created in the 1980s to help perpetuate the memory of the league. They have associate members, those who did not play or who were born long after the league had ended play. The combination of those two groups will ensure the memory and action of the AAGPBL for all time.

This is a 1954 season pass for the South Bend Blue Sox games at Playland Park. This was the final regular season of play for the All-American Girls Professional Baseball League. Officials from the league decided to suspend play for 1955, and games never did resume.

"I Want to Be A Lassie When I Grow Up"

This image is from the 1948 Muskegon Lassies yearbook. The young girl pictured here had the same dreams and aspirations to play baseball in the AAAGPBL as many of her favorite players.

At left is Connie "Iron Woman" Wisniewski and catcher Ruth "Tex" Lessing. Wisniewski was one of the AAGPBL's most durable pitchers in the first few seasons when underhand pitching was used. Lessing was a fan favorite, one time getting her league fine paid by the fans following an altercation she had with one of the umpires.

In this photograph from 1948, Ruth "Tex" Lessing is shown putting on make-up while waiting to take a turn at bat. During the first season of the AAGPBL, players attended a charm school.

One of the most popular players in the history of the AAGPBL was Mary "Bonnie" Baker. As a member of the South Bend Blue Sox, she is seen here at Playland Park instructing a young boy on the fine art of catching.

This is the 1947 program cover for the South Bend Blue Sox. One of the marketing strategies used during most of the seasons for the AAGPBL's existence was the use of identical program and scorecard covers. The only differences would be the team name and color.

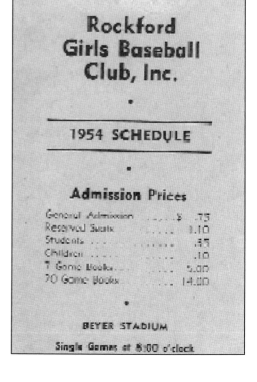

Here is the 1954 list of admission prices to attend a Rockford Peaches home game at Beyer Stadium. Rockford and South Bend were the only two teams to play the entire span of the AAGPBL (1943–54).

Here is the program for the 1949 Fort Wayne Daisies. That season, the team would be managed by Harold Greiner. Some of the top talent that season included June Peppas, Kay Blumetta, and Dottie Schroeder.

This photograph was taken during the AAGPBL spring training in Miami, FL. Sliding is Sophie Kurys of Racine, and attempting to put the tag on her is Ruth "Tex" Lessing, catcher for Grand Rapids.

This is the 1947 yearbook cover from the Muskegon Lassies. In 1946, their first season in Muskegon, the team drew nearly 90,000 to Marsh Field. In 1947, the team was managed by former Brooklyn Dodger outfielder Ralph "Buzz" Boyle. Two of the top players on the team were Alva Jo "Tex" Fischer who hit .309 in 1946 and Doris "Sammy" Sams who hit .274.

During the time period of the AAGPBL, there were a number of images that were meant to be a tongue-in-cheek commentary about female baseball players. This postcard is from 1947 and is titled "Hit and Miss."

Perhaps though, the best known of the images that poked fun at the female ballplayers was this Varga print from 1944. The short verse in the upper right hand of the image, written by Phil Stack, is titled "All-American Babe," and reads:

The war has made some changes
In our nation's fav'rite game,
For 'teen kids are making
A bid for baseball fame
And though these "All-American Boys"
Will star as sure as fate,
We'll add an "All-American Babe"
And overflow the gate.

The Major League of Girls Baseball

ALL-AMERICAN GIRLS

462 WRIGLEY BUILDING, CHICAGO, ILL.

(Copyright, 1948, by All-American Girls Baseball League Advisory Board)

FRED K. LEO, President

An Association of Eight Member Clubs owned and operated by local civic and industrial leaders on a community, non-profit basis, at:

Rockford, Illinois
South Bend, Indiana
Grand Rapids, Michigan
Racine, Wisconsin
Peoria, Illinois
Fort Wayne, Indiana
Muskegon, Michigan
Kenosha, Wisconsin

Chicago Colleens and Springfield Sallies
Travelling Teams

Big League Operation

● The best player talent is scouted and recommended by qualified Commissioners covering the United States, Canada and Cuba. Winter tryout schools for new players are conducted from coast to coast. Farm and affiliated leagues are used for development of talent.

New prospects are signed to a tryout agreement which protects amateur standing before a definite contract is offered to turn pro. Players are rated and assigned to teams on the basis of a rating chart and a point system which charts ability in all phases of the game. Players are distributed to the ten clubs by the league to assure equitable balance and even competition. New and exclusive Total Advanced Bases column records actual performance of individual players. All league players receive a complete course in fundamentals at spring training camp.

This is the first and only league to train all of its clubs at one spring training site, in such glamorous settings as Pascagoula, Mississippi; Havana, Cuba; Opa-Locka, Florida in recent years, with all expenses paid by the league. And it is the only girls professional league playing this special and exclusive brand of baseball in the world today.

● All-American girls come from all parts of the United States, Canada and Cuba. They are selected for their athletic and baseball ability as well as femininity, character and deportment. A high standard of conduct and behavior is maintained at all times. Players live in private homes in their home town. On the road, first class of the best hotels. All travelling expenses and meal expenses on the road are paid by the club. Weekly salaries range from $55.00 to $100.00 per week. Players become an important part of the civic and social life of the community. Games are attended by the best youth element in all communities, including men, women, boys and girls, with single game crowds as large as 5,000 to 10,000 people. Girls baseball is the most widely publicized and best attended sport in the league cities, back from has a maximum roster of 15 players, a manager and chaperone. The individual club operations are managed by a board of directors comprising the top business and civic leaders in the community, with a business manager, official scorer, field announcer and all the facilities and services in the best tradition of big league baseball. Travel by air and private bus, play-by-play radio and television broadcasts are some of the more recent indications of the growing greatness of girls baseball as a top sport of the nation.

This promotional flyer was produced by the AAGPBL offices in Chicago, IL. The flyer (from 1948) shows the locations for the then ten clubs that made up the league. It gives a brief

70

.BALL LEAGUE

NE MOHAWK 4-0538-4-0539

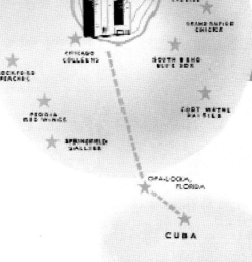

This internationally publicized game has quadrupled its attendance in five years, with 1948 attendance topping the 900,000 mark.

It is *not* softball, but actual *baseball*, with its own exclusive rules and features . . . 72-foot basepaths, 55-foot pitching distance, 10-inch horsehide baseball, base stealing and *baseball* rules.

Each team is led by a selected, qualified and experienced manager with years of major and minor league *baseball* experience and know-how, including some of the most famous players of all time.

Each team is assigned a chaperone who is responsible for conditioning, first aid, uniforms and equipment, living and travel arrangements, general health, welfare and deportment.

All games are handled by the double umpire system with a full-time staff of qualified, experienced and completely uniformed umpires and officials.

All team personnel play *baseball* exclusively as a full-time occupation in a schedule of 112 games per season, with 56 home games and 56 road games in the seven other league cities, under the lights in modern, attractive, up-to-date stadia and *baseball* parks.

With two teams operating in four States in the general area surrounding Chicago and Lake Michigan, travel and playing conditions are pleasant and inviting. Starting in 1946, the entire league personnel has trained en masse at such numerous southern locations as Pascagoula, Havana and Opa-locka, near Miami, Florida. In 1948, the ten teams played spring championship series in Havana, Tampa, Daytona Beach, Miami, Miami Beach and many other southern cities. Summer time living and travel in the Lake Michigan resort area is pleasant and enjoyable.

description of the rules, salaries, and basic operation.

This is the 1952 scorecard from the Grand Rapids Chicks. Grand Rapids had a team in the AAGPBL from 1946 through the 1954 season. In 1953, they won their only league championship.

Many former major leaguers managed teams during the course of the history of the AAGPBL. But only one of those managers (Max Carey) went on to serve as president of the league as well.

Pictured here in 1946 is Irene Ruhnke, the second sacker for the Fort Wayne Daisies. One of the standout stars of the AAGPBL, scouting reports touted her as having "a strong arm and plenty of punch at the plate."

This is a 1947 Kenosha Comets' program cover. Kenosha was a member of the AAGPBL from its inception in 1943 until 1951. In 1943 and 1944, the Comets would either capture the first or second half season division championship, but never won a league title. Many players joked about the fog that would sometimes roll off of Lake Michigan into the outfield at Lakefront Stadium. Sometimes, the players said, "You couldn't see the person next to you and that made a fly ball in the outfield an interesting adventure!"

This is a scorecard cover from the Peoria (IL) Redwings, who were members of the AAGPBL from 1946-51. Their best season was in 1948 when they won 70 games and only lost 55.

Sophie Kurys is perhaps the greatest base stealer of all-time. In just eight seasons in the AAGPBL, she stole 1,114 bases. Known as the "Flint Flash," in 1946 Sophie stole 201 bases in 203 attempts and was voted Player of the Year.

This scorecard is from the Muskegon Lassies, c. 1947. Like many scorecards found at ballparks today, a fan would be able to check a roster, keep score, and of course, see if the Lucky Number stamped inside would be a winner for them.

The "Tops In Girls Sports" brochure was one of the many publicity tools used by the AAGPBL offices. Inside of the brochure, fans could find out where teams were located, where spring trainings were held, and what kinds of salaries were paid to the players.

ALL AMERICAN GIRLS BASEBALL LEAGUE

The All American Girls Baseball League, on the eve of it's sixth season, of play, has become an internationally accepted game, packed with action and thrills and providing clean, wholesome entertainment to over a million fans annually.

It has truly become the fastest growing spectator sport in America and this record is due to a large extent to the fact that the teams are staffed by the finest young feminine athletes obtainable. The ten teams comprising the league are governed by a board of directors from each of the ten cities represented and these directors are accepted civic leaders and recognized business and professional men in their own community.

Each team operates as a non-profit corporation, as does the overall league organization, and the directors are non-salaried. All profits accruing from the regular 126 game season are dedicated to municipal playground and youth recreational work in the league cities. This game has proved to be a factor in combating juvenile delinquency wherever it is played.

It is real baseball, not to be confused with softball, and overall baseball rules govern at all times. The diamond has been slightly scaled down to allow for the speed differences between men and women. The distance between bases is 72 feet and the pitcher throws from a mound 48 feet from home plate. The ball used is a horsehide covered baseball, made to the same specifications as the major league standard ball with the only exception that the girls baseball is 1-3/8 inches larger in circumference.

The girls are managed by such former major league stars as Dave Bancroft, Johnny Rawlings, Marty McManus, Bill Wamby, and Carson Bigbee, all of whom work under the direction of League President Max Carey. The girls come from all parts of the United States, Canada, and Cuba. Some of the girls are faculty members of the athletic departments of leading colleges and universities; others are secretarial and clerical workers, school teachers, salesladies, and some are just "Mrs. Housewife" during the off season. The girls average anywhere from $55.00 to $100.00 per week, depending upon playing records and length of service.

This is another type of information piece used by the AAGPBL. This particular one is from 1948. Once the teams began to operate as independent entities, promotional material like this would be left to those individual teams.

Pictured here is Jo Weaver from the Fort Wayne Daisies. She played in the AAGPBL from 1951 to 1954. She was considered a solid player in the field and at bat.

A 1950 program and scorecard for the Fort Wayne Daisies is pictured here. That season, Max Carey managed the team. Under Carey, the team finished with a record of 62-43, second only to the league champion Rockford Peaches.

There has probably never been a greater group of fans than those who were followers of the AAGPBL. Players were taken into and became part of the communities in which they played. Many times, unique, homemade gifts would be taken to the ballpark and given to a favorite player. Pictured here is a c. 1944 wooden folk art plaque that features two AAGPBL players from the Racine Belles.

Following the end of the AAGPBL, a touring team of former players was organized by Bill Allington. This team is from the 1958 season. Much like the old-time Bloomer Girls, this team traveled many miles and played against male teams. The hope was that with enough publicity, the AAGPBL might restart and expand to more cities. On this 1958 team were,

from left to right, Bill Allington, Mgr., Joanne Weaver, Dottie Schroeder, Katie Horstman, Joan Eisenberger, Gertie Dunn, Ruth Richard, Dolores Lee, Jean Smith, Jean Geissinger, and Maxine Kline.

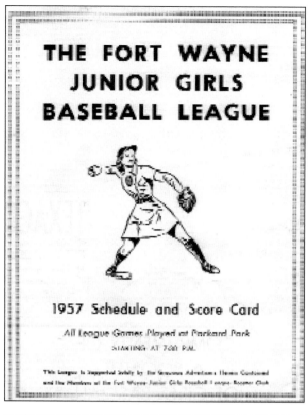

THE FORT WAYNE JUNIOR GIRLS BASEBALL LEAGUE

1957 Schedule and Score Card

All League Games Played at Packard Park
STARTING AT 7:00 P.M.

This League is supported solely by the Suncrest Adventure Heroes Contained and the Members of the Fort Wayne Junior Girls Baseball League Booster Club

One of the legacies left by the AAGPBL was the belief that girls could play baseball, and play it well. Many cities in the league helped develop youth baseball programs for girls. This is a 1957 program from the Fort Wayne Junior Girls Baseball League.

This is a photograph of the Redwings team that played in the Fort Wayne Junior Girls Baseball League. With their roots in the AAGPBL, Fort Wayne has continued to offer a baseball program for girls for over 50 years.

FOUR

Chasing Baseball Dreams 1957–2004

Following the end of the All-American Girls Professional Baseball League in 1954, female baseball players would still be in the news from time to time. However, there were few attempts at organizing leagues for either girls or women.

The City of Fort Wayne, IN, was one of the few cities in the United States to continue to have a baseball program geared toward girls. When a Pawtucket, RI Little League did not allow a girl by the name of Alison "Pookie" Fortin to play baseball, a group of parents started the Pawtucket Saturates Girls Baseball League (1973). The League is still in operation today. In the early 1970s, Little League eventually created a softball program for girls (and in 2000 one for boys as well), but the organization hasn't made any efforts to create and promote a separate baseball program for girls.

In the late 1970s, some women's baseball leagues briefly popped up but did not last. In the 1980s, one organization, the American Women's Baseball Association (AWBA) created the first long-lived women's baseball organization since the All-American League.

Organized by Darlene A. Mehrer in 1988, the organization competed for 14 seasons. Based in the suburban area around Chicago, as many as five teams played during any one season.

In November of 1988, the National Baseball Hall of Fame in Cooperstown, New York opened its first permanent exhibition on the role of women in baseball. Much of the exhibit was dedicated to the players of the All-American League. Hundreds of former players, their families, and friends attended the dedication.

Just a few years after AWBA was launched, the 1992 hit movie *A League of Their Own* excited a new generation of baseball players and fans. While giving their due to the pioneer players of the AAGPBL, new competitive doors were opened for women as baseball players. Amateur leagues began to spring up all around the country. Currently, the oldest operating amateur baseball league in the United States is the Eastern Women's Baseball Conference. The Conference, first known as the Washington Metropolitan Women's Baseball League, was founded by Lydia Moon and was modeled after the Chicago area AWBA.

Professionally, the Coors Brewing Company held tryouts and created a traveling women's baseball team, the Silver Bullets (playing from 1994 to 1997). They were originally managed by Phil Niekro. The Ladies Pro Baseball League began play in 1997 as a West Coast organization and in 1998, they expanded to the East Coast as well. But by the middle of the season, the league folded due to financial difficulties.

Other amateur leagues and organizations continued to materialize. During the winter of 1996, Jim Glennie, organizer of the Michigan Women's Baseball League, teamed with Joe Cooper of the American Amateur Baseball League (AABC) and USA Baseball, Inc. to help create the Great Lakes Women's Baseball League. In a circuit similar to that of the old All-American League, the cities of South Bend and Fort Wayne, Indiana, Chicago, Illinois along with Battle Creek and Lansing, Michigan made up the league that first season. In 2005, The League celebrates its 10th anniversary. The Women's Baseball League was organized in 1997 by Justine Siegal and based in Ohio. Since that time, the organization (although still based in Ohio) has been more involved with girl's and women's baseball in Toronto, Canada.

In 2001, Glennie, president of the Women's International Baseball Association helped to co-ordinate the first-ever Women's Baseball World Series in Toronto, Canada. Glennie worked with Tom Giffen of Roy Hobbs Baseball, Inc. (whose organization hosts the Women's Baseball National Championship each fall in Fort Myers, FL) to help set-up nationwide tryouts to pick a U.S. women's baseball team that would represent the U.S. The Series, won by the U.S., featured teams from host Canada as well as Australia and Japan.

During the 2003 season, baseball teams in the U.S. worked on becoming part of Amateur Athletic Union (AAU). During this trial period, the numbers of players and teams grew and in the fall of 2003, women's baseball became an official sanctioned sport of AAU. They work in helping to co-sponsor the Women's National Championship hosted by Roy Hobbs Baseball. A new Boston area women's baseball organization, the North American Women's Baseball League, began play in 2003. Four teams played in their first season and the same number played again in the local league in 2004.

USA Baseball, Inc. in 2004 again became involved with women's baseball as they helped pick a team to participate in both the Women's World Series, hosted by Japan and the Women's World Cup, played in Edmonton, Canada.

The United States finished second in the World Series and first in the World Cup games.

The Saturday Evening

POST

April 21, 1951 — 15¢

A young girl kicks and gets ready to deliver a pitch to a batter. This magazine cover is from *The Saturday Evening Post*, dated April 21, 1951. This rendering is just another example of female baseball players who have appeared in various publications since before the turn of the century.

The issue of integration was never dealt with in the AAGPBL. The Negro Leagues integrated on a couple of different levels by signing a number of female baseball players and later, white players to play in the league. Pictured here is infielder Toni Stone. In 1953 and 1954, she played for both the Indianapolis Clowns and the Kansas City Monarchs.

In 1948, 19-year-old Beatrice Metes caused quite a stir being a pitcher on the St. Joseph American Legion baseball team in Joliet, Illinois. She is pictured here with her manager, Ed Briese. Beatrice's brother Rob is the regular catch for the team.

Even years ago, a good ballplayer needed to have iron rich blood. This *c.* 1955 ad for Bosco Milk Amplifier uses an enthusiastic young female hitter (along with the young boy who is catching) to help make their point.

This *c.* 1950 valentine shows a young skirted hitter. Her outfit contains some similarity to those worn by the AAGPBL players (with the exception of the flowers in front).

In 1955, over 700 girls between the ages of eight and 14 played baseball in Massapequa Park in Long Island, New York. In this photograph, coach Larry Neusse teaches the basics of sliding.

This Aluminum Limited ad from 1958 shows how newer school buildings contain the lightweight, but durable aluminum trim. Testing the durability is a young female baseball player who has launched a ball to test that metal.

One of the biggest moments for women's baseball came in the fall of 1988, when *Women In Baseball*, a permanent exhibit, was dedicated at the National Baseball Hall of Fame in Cooperstown, New York.

In the early 1990s, the Women's Baseball Association began play in Florida. Even though the association did not last very long, Florida still has strong teams (like Ocala and Jacksonville) that play in various tournaments. Plans are underway to launch a new Florida Women's Baseball League in 2005.

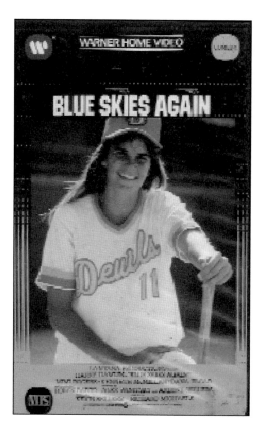

The theme of women and baseball is also found in movies other than *A League of Their Own*. This story is about Paula Franklin and her dream of playing in the major leagues with the Denver Devils. The movie was summed up this way: "It's the most enjoyable baseball comedy since *Damn Yankees* taught us about the essential ingredient of heart."

Sue Lukasik played for a number of years in the Great lakes Women's Baseball League and served as president of the Chicago-area AWBA. When she wasn't playing baseball, she spent time acting as an extra at Wrigley Field during the filming of *A League of Their Own*. This is her baseball card commemorating that movie experience.

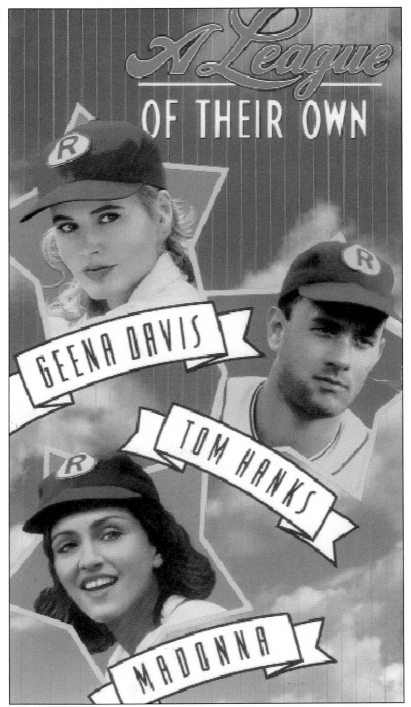

This is the promotional poster for the 1992 movie, *A League of Their Own*. The movie not only helped recognize the pioneer players of the AAGPBL, it also rekindled an interest in women and girls baseball. Many players today can recite any given line of the movie, from any scene, and it's not difficult to find a dugout where at least one time during a game a line from the movie is used.

In 1994, the Coors Brewing Company launched a professional women's baseball team called the Colorado Silver Bullets. Pictured here is Julie Croteau who was the first female to play NCAA baseball at the Division III St. Mary's College of Maryland. She also served as a coach on the first-ever National Women's Baseball Team picked in 2004 by USA Baseball.

The Silver Bullets gave Gina Satriano a chance to play the game she loved. Satriano was the first female to play Little League Baseball in California. When the chance to play with the Silver Bullets came along, she left a highly successful law practice to follow her dream.

Beginning in 1993, the South Florida Diamond League began play. At one time, they were the largest women's baseball league in Florida with eight teams in a three county area. A number of the players from the league can still be found on the baseball diamonds around the country.

"More Than Just Baseball"

1994 · 95 SEASON

BRIAN PICCOLO PARK
9501 Sheridan Street
Cooper City, Florida

Currently, the Eastern Women's Baseball Conference is the senior operating women's baseball league in the United States. The can trace their beginnings back to 1990, when they were known as the Washington Metropolitan Women's Baseball League. This program cover is from their 10th anniversary tournament in 1999.

Patty "Mayo" George comes to her set position on the mound during a tournament at Stanley Coveleski regional Stadium in South Bend. During her career she has played for AWBA and the Great Lakes League for the South Bend and the Chicago Storm. While at medical school in Baltimore, Maryland, George continued playing in the Washington Metropolitan Women's Baseball League.

This photograph was taken during a baseball game in 1996 at Oldsmobile Park in Lansing, MI. The batter is a member of the Lansing Stars and the catcher is Sue Lukasik of the South Bend Belles. Both were members of the Great Lakes Women's Baseball League during its inaugural season in 1996.

When the Colorado Silver Bullets were formed, their first manager was Phil Niekro. Over the years, Niekro became a big supporter of women who wanted to play baseball and said his hardest task was cutting down to the final roster. He said that unlike the major leagues, there was no minor league system. When you were cut—there really was no place to go. Niekro is pictured here during a 1996 visit by the Silver Bullets to Oldsmobile Park.

In 2001, the United States, along with Australia, Canada and Japan, competed in the first-ever Women's Baseball World Series, which was held in Toronto, Canada. This photograph shows the U.S. Team ready for opening ceremonies. Holding the Team USA banner on the left is Ashley Oliver and on the right, Emily Kovach.

On the right, Emily Kovach takes a picture with Ila Borders who was taking a break from a girl's baseball clinic. Borders, a left-handed pitcher, was a scholarship baseball player at the NAIA, South California College. She is wearing the jersey from the Northern League St. Paul Saints, an independent minor league team for whom she had played for that past season.

In 2001, women's baseball came to Tiger stadium in Detroit, MI. Although it had been closed for a number of seasons, two women's games were played on August 11, 2001. Teams featured that day were the Detroit Danger and Toronto International All-Stars in the first game and the Patriot All-Stars and the American All-Stars in game two. The event was organized by the WBL.

Carrying on a baseball tradition that dated back to 1905 at her Saint Mary's College campus, Dawn Tuel from Denton, MD (a 2004 Saint Mary's graduate) played a number of tournament games as a member of the South Bend Blue Sox. She also placed in the top 10 of a winter high school baseball hitting league her freshman year.

Today in women's baseball tournaments, there is always an opportunity for players to play even if their own regular season team doesn't play in those events. One such team was the Great Lakes Fire who played in 2002 at the Roy Hobbs Women's National Championship in Ft. Myers, FL. Team members included, from left to right: (front row) Irina Kovach (Indiana) and at left Clayton Beining (Florida); (middle row) Amy Schneider (Illinois), Kelly Rodman (Connecticut), Tammy Johnson (Ohio), Brenda Moors (Ohio) and Vanessa West (Pennsylvania); (back row) Sally Potter (Michigan), Christen Williams (Illinois), Sandy Maurer (Ohio), Tina Beining (Florida), and John Kovach, manager (Indiana).

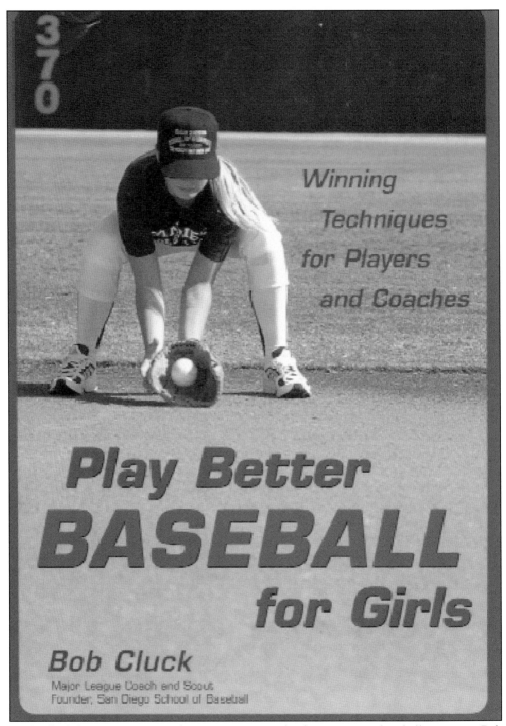

Winning Techniques for Players and Coaches

Play Better BASEBALL for Girls

Bob Cluck

Major League Coach and Scout
Founder, San Diego School of Baseball

With all of the young women who were coming to his hitting camp, baseball instructor Bob Cluck wrote a baseball coaching book for girls. By all accounts, it had been probably almost 70 years since the last book geared toward teaching the game of baseball to girls had been written. Besides his hitting school, Cluck has also been on a number of major league coaching staffs.

One of the most durable pitchers in the Great Lakes Women's Baseball League is Kris Raniszewski. A lefty, Kris works from the middle of the plate out and away. Just when the batter feels that they can crowd the plate on her, she will buzz a fastball in tight on them. Raniszewski has played for the Michigan Stars, Detroit Danger, and Motown Magic.

At the opening of a 2003 museum exhibit, *Women In Sports—Breaking Barriers*, Ashley Holderman of the South end Blue Sox (left) and Carol Sheldon of the Detroit Danger, pause for a photo opportunity near the Playland Park sign in the exhibit area devoted to the AAGPBL.

During the opening of *Women In Sports—Breaking Barriers*, a large number of former AAGPBL players were in town for both the exhibit and for a mini-reunion in South Bend. Some of the current baseball players take an opportunity to meet with a player who helped change the face

of women's sports. From left to right are Janet Smith (Saint Mary's College), Gloria Cordes Elliott (AAGPBL), Ericka Johnson (Mishawaka High School), and Katie Pappa (Lakeshore High School).

Perhaps no player in women's baseball is more recognizable today that Molly McKesson. The 19-year-old right-handed pitcher has been a member of every U.S. women's baseball team that has played in the World Series. Her solid work as a high school pitcher has led her to Christian Brothers University in Memphis, TN, where she becomes the first female to receive a baseball scholarship at an NCAA school. (Photograph courtesy of Molly McKesson.)

Katie Pappa of the South Bend Blue Sox crouches to get ready for a pitch during the 2004 season. Pappa, who is 16, has been playing for the Blue Sox since she was 13 years old. On defense, she can usually be found behind the plate, at shortstop or third base or on the mound. At age 14, she became the youngest National MVP (an award presented by the National Women's Baseball Hall of Fame in Chevy Chase, Maryland). That season she hit .400 and led her team in hits, doubles, and runs batted in.

Teammate Katie Pappa (left) and Christine Molnar make their way off the infield at the end of an inning. A number of times during the 2004 season, they formed the double play combination for the South Bend Blue Sox. Pappa played short and Molnar played second.

Katy Smythe, a solid, all-around infielder and pitcher was chosen for the 2001 women's baseball team that represented the United States at the first annual Women's World Series. Smythe has been a participant at the Detroit Tigers' fantasy camps. This card, from her 2001 camp showed her hitting .500 (6 for 12) to go along with a 1-0 pitching record.

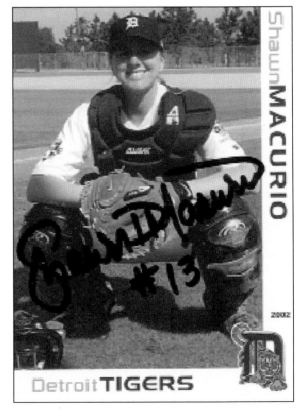

Another Tigers' fantasy camp attendee is Shawn Macurio, organizer and general manager of the Detroit Danger of the Great Lakes Women's Baseball League since 2000. Macurio plays infield, pitches, and catches for the Danger. However, the past several off seasons have found her participating in the Tigers' camp. In 2002, she made her pitching debut in big time fashion. After pitching only one inning in her life beforehand, Macurio finished with a camp record of 3-0 with two saves and an earned run average of 0.50.

D'Andre Christian has played both infield and outfield for the South Bend Blue Sox since joining the team in 2001. Christian smacked five hits and drove in four runs in the opening season doubleheader.

South Bend Blue Sox manager John Kovach and Chicago Gems outfielder Christen Williams discuss a game situation. Often times for tournaments, players from different teams and leagues will join together to play in theses games.

One of the most feared base runners in women's baseball is Jenn "Taz" Hughes from the Chicago Storm. During her career, she has stolen bases at a success rate of over 90 percent. Her mere presence on the base paths often forces the opposition into mistakes.

Ashley Holderman has been a member of the South Bend Blue Sox since 1997. She opted not to play her remaining year for her high school softball time in order to work on her baseball pitching mechanics. An outstanding defensive player, Holderman played four straight seasons of errorless ball despite the fact she saw action at seven different positions.

An Ocala Lightning base runner lies prone on the ground after being stopped in her bid to score. Pitcher Ashley Holderman covered and blocked the plate on the run attempt and now jogs back to her bench.

Over the years, the former players of the AAGPBL have been honored at many different ballparks. In 1989, a number of the All-Americans were recognized by the South Bend White Sox minor league ball club. In this photograph, then South Bend Mayor Joe Kernan (with Sox general manager John Baxter right behind him) presents a certificate to Lou Arnold as another former player, Janet "Pee Wee" Sears, looks on.

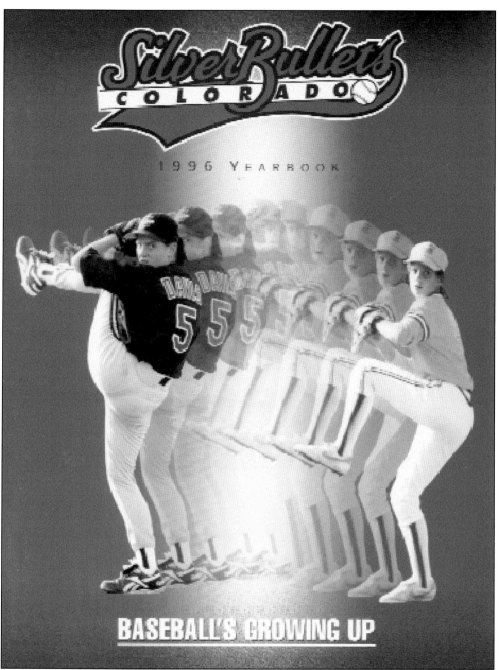

SilverBullets
COLORADO

1996 YEARBOOK

BASEBALL'S GROWING UP

In 1994, the Coors Brewing Company started a professional women's baseball team, the Colorado Silver Bullets. The club traveled all over the United States playing men's amateur and semi-pro teams. At the end of 1997 however, Coors dropped its team sponsorship on the reasoning that they didn't want to have consumers think that their product was a women's beer.

Sarah Ward played infield for the South Bend Blue Sox in 1999–01. She spent most of her time at either third base or shortstop. Ward joined the team when she was 16 years old. Her first season she set a team record for chances at shortstop during a single game, handling 13 opportunities without an error.

Blue Sox hitter Sarah Ward waits for her pitch at the plate during a 2001 tournament at Stanley Coveleski Regional Stadium. In her three seasons with the team, she hit for averages of .316, .314, and .315.

This *Highlights for Children* magazine from May of 1996 continues a tradition of earlier children's magazines that depict the image of a young girl playing baseball.

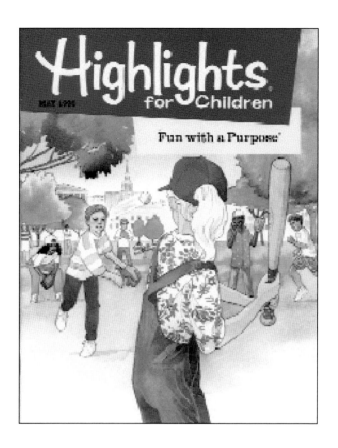

This is a ticket form a 1996 Great Lakes Women's Baseball League doubleheader between the South Bend Belles and Lansing Stars that was played at Oldsmobile Park in Lansing, MI. The 1996 season was the first year for the Great Lakes League that was organized by Jim Glennie with the help of USA Baseball, Inc. and the American Amateur Baseball Congress (AABC).

In 1998, the National Women's Baseball Hall of Fame was established in Chevy Chase, MD. Its goal is to be able to support the achievements of women who play regulation baseball. National MVPs and managerial awards as well as awards for baseball skills are part of the honors given out by the National Women's Baseball Hall of Fame. Pictured here is a commemorative patch from the first year Hall of Fame inductions..

It was only fitting that the first active player to receive membership into the National Women's Baseball Hall of Fame was pitcher Charlene Wright. In 1999, Wright and former AAGPBL player Claire Schillace of the Racine Belles (1943–46) were the first two inductees. Wright is one of the most durable pitchers to ever play women's baseball. If you take her average amount of games and innings during the course of a season and project them over a 162 game schedule, she would average over 400 innings pitched. Over the course of some of the major women's baseball tournaments (lasting three to four days), it's not unusual to see her log over 20 innings of work.

Joni Stegeman played 12 seasons of Little League Baseball in the Skokie Indians (Illinois) organization. In her first official at bat, she cracked a grandslam. It was just a sign of things to come. Stegeman, an infielder/pitcher, has played for the Chicago Storm of the Great Lakes Women's Baseball League. At age 17, she was one of the youngest players selected in 2001 for the US women's baseball team that played in the inaugural Women's World Series.

Donna Mills (shown here at third base) was selected for the Women's World Series team in 2001. One of the toughest hitters in women's baseball, she is no slouch with the glove either.

Most of her career has been spent with teams in the New England area.

One of the perks of playing women's baseball is the opportunity to travel to many different cities over the course of a season. In this photograph, three members of the South Bend Blue Sox enjoy an afternoon in Washington, DC, during a 1999 Labor Day tournament. From left to right are Mary Ann Slinn, Amy Mazner, and Melanie Carter.

Carol Sheldon of the Great Lakes Stars waits on a pitch during a 2001 tourney. Sheldon has played in the Great Lakes Women's Baseball League for the Lansing Stars, Detroit Danger, and Motown Magic as well as playing on the Great Lakes Stars and South Bend Blue Sox tournament teams. She is one of the most knowledgeable players in the game as well as being a solid teacher of the game of baseball.

Dirt on Their Skirts

THE STORY OF THE YOUNG WOMEN WHO WON THE WORLD CHAMPIONSHIP

Doreen Rappaport ✦ Lyndall Callan

PICTURES BY *E. B. Lewis*

Published in 2000, *Dirt on Their Skirts*, by Doreen Rappaport and Lyndall Callan, tells the story of a fictitious family who are rooting for the hometown Racine Belles in their 1946 All-American Girls Baseball League championship game against the Rockford Peaches (which really took place). Although the family in the story is not real, based on countless conversations with former fans of the AAGPBL, there is no doubt that the strong feelings of the fans are well-spoken for in this book. Racine topped Rockford in that game by a score a 1-0 before a total crowd of 5,603.

Third baseman Ashley Nicolls starts to move back toward the bag to catch a base runner from the Florida Crush who has wandered too far off base. Nicolls hails from Hibbing, Minnesota and has played for a number of women's baseball tournament teams over the past five seasons.

While at first base, Ashley Nicolls looks down for a sign from her coach across the diamond. Yasmin Fatah (#2) is in the first base coaching box. The defensive player is from the Florida Crush.

Yasmin Fatah holds the ball at second base after narrowly missing the tag out of a runner from the Jacksonville (FL) Flames. In the background, shortstop Katie Pappa looks on.

First base coach Andi Ermis (with shin guards) attempts to help runner Ashley Nicolls with her lead off of first. The opposing first baseman is from the Ocala Lightning.

Kelly Jewell of the South Bend Blue Sox tosses her bat away after getting a base on balls. In 2004, Jewell was named a National MVP by the National Women's Baseball Hall of Fame. During the course of the season, Jewell hit .565 while leading her team in at bats, runs, and hits. She also was perfect in 13 stolen base attempts and played errorless ball in the outfield.

South Bend Blue Sox catcher Lori Bryant looks down to third to see if the hit or take sign is on. Bryant also was named a National MVP for her play this past season. In 2004, she hit .476, led the team in doubles and knocked in 10 runs. She compiled a pitching record of 3-1, and defensively while in back of the plate she threw out 68 percent of the would be base runners.

GIRL WONDER

A Baseball Story in Nine Innings

by DEBORAH HOPKINSON
with pictures by TERRY WIDENER

This book, *Girl Wonder*, was published in 2003. It tells the story of Alta Weiss, an outstanding female pitcher in the early 1990s. From the money she made from her skills as a baseball pitcher, she was able to put herself through medical school and became an outstanding doctor. It's a great book about a phenomenal woman.

Ten-year-old Marina Kovach gets ready to toss the baseball back to an instructor during a clinic at Stanley Coveleski Regional Stadium in July of 2004. Marina, a New York Yankees fan, and her twin sister Irina were among seven girls who participated in the clinic that was put on by the Midwest League South Bend Silver Hawks.

Irina Kovach starts to position herself for a fly ball drill during a clinic at Coveleski Stadium. Kovach has played two years of baseball at the New Prairie Little League in New Carlisle. In 2003, she was the only girl playing baseball at the park, but in 2004, she was joined on her team by her twin sister Marina.

Catcher Robin Wallace starts a walk to the mound for a chat with her pitcher. Wallace, a veteran baseball performer, can be found pitching, catching, or in the infield depending on where her team needs her most. For the past several seasons, she has played with various teams in the Boston area. In 2003, she was named as the executive director for the North American Women's Baseball League.

In 2003, the New England Women's Baseball League was given a financial boost by businessman Nicholas A. Lopardo. Through his efforts a four-team league and a tournament travel team was created. The League provided for all of the players' equipment needs, including the use of Fraser Field in Lynn, MA for their games. A number of the players who played that summer either worked at Fraser Field or were found jobs in the local community. The League was a success and operated for a second year with four teams in the Boston area.

Although Robin Wallace relishes and enjoys her role as executive director of the North American Women's Baseball League, she still prefers to compete on the diamond. In this photograph, the switch-hitting Wallace is batting left handed and has just started her swing.

Beyer Stadium in Rockford, IL, played home to many baseball games in the course of its history. Built in 1923 at a cost of $30,452, it was well-known as the home of the Rockford Peaches of the AAGPBL during their 12-year run. This commemorative tin was being sold to help raise finds to build a new ballpark on the site of the old stadium.

This 1979 tale of *The Great Pete Penney* by Jean Bashor Tolle, tells of an 11-year-old girl who is the only female on her baseball team and how she longs to throw a curveball that no one can hit. She meets-up with Mike McGlory (who is all of six inches tall) who helps Penney throw that special curve. Her team, the Blue Sox, then wins the pennant and gets a chance to play an exhibition game at Wrigley Field.

The California Sabres are the traveling tournament team from the Southern California Women's Baseball League. Pictured here are members of the 2003 Sabres. Pictured from left to right are: (front row) Sharon Martin, Bernie Vaughn, Rhonda Valdez, Kelly Deutsch, and Cherie Leatherwood; (middle row) Chris Hill, Tammy Treat, Amber Kerns, Cindy Ross, Kim Hoover, and Melanie Betti; (top row) Pam Conro, Heather Lindsey, Steph Torres, Stephanie Sharp, Alison Maya, Stefanie Young, and Sabrina Sexton.

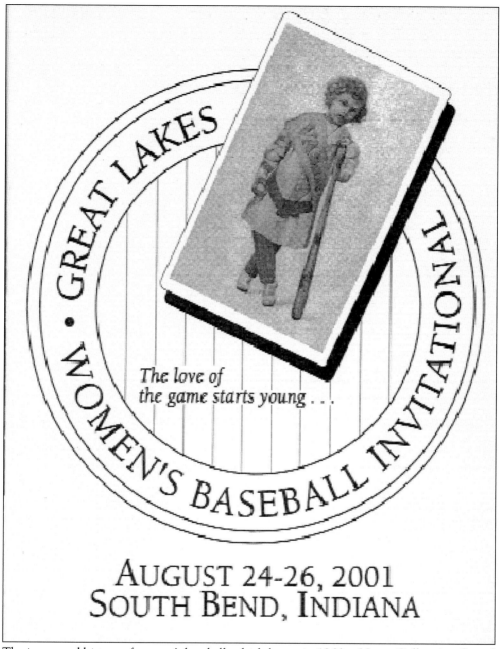

The love of
the game starts young . . .

GREAT LAKES · WOMEN'S BASEBALL INVITATIONAL

AUGUST 24-26, 2001
SOUTH BEND, INDIANA

The image and history of women's baseball, which began in 1866 at Vassar College is reflected in this 2001 Great Lakes Women's Baseball Invitational program. The design for this program (and tournament shirt) was created by Curt Sochocki, senior graphic artist at Saint Mary's College, Notre Dame, Indiana.

South Bend Blue Sox batgirl Irina Kovach casually blows a bubble while waiting to hop into action. When not working during the summer as a batgirl, Kovach can be found playing infield or catching for her Little League team and rooting for her favorite major league team, the Boston Red Sox.